Crayola

Crayola
SPRING COLORS

Jodie Shepherd

Lerner Publications ◆ Minneapolis

Official Licensed Product
Lerner Publications Company
A division of Lerner Publishing Group, Inc.
241 First Avenue North
Minneapolis, MN 55401 USA

For reading levels and more information, look up this title at www.lernerbooks.com.

Main body text set in Billy Infant Regular 24/36.
Typeface provided by SparkyType.

Library of Congress Cataloging-in-Publication Data

Names: Shepherd, Jodie.
Title: Crayola spring colors / by Jodie Shepherd.
Description: Minneapolis : Lerner Publications, [2018] | Series: Crayola
  seasons | Audience: Age 4-9. | Audience: K to grade 3. | Includes bibliographical
    references and index.
Identifiers: LCCN 2016044743 (print) | LCCN 2016045541 (ebook) | ISBN
  9781512432923 (lb : alk. paper) | ISBN 9781512455748 (pb : alk. paper) | ISBN
  9781512449303 (eb pdf)
Subjects: LCSH: Spring—Juvenile literature. | Seasons—Juvenile literature. | Crayons—
  Juvenile literature.
Classification: LCC QB637.5 .S54 2018 (print) | LCC QB637.5 (ebook) | DDC 535.6—dc23

LC record available at https://lccn.loc.gov/2016044743

Manufactured in the United States of America
1-41823-23783-1/23/2017

TABLE OF CONTENTS

NATURE IN SPRINGTIME

Spring is here! The weather gets warmer. Outside you find fresh green grass, a yellow sun, and bright pink blossoms.

Look around!

5

Even before the snow has all melted, flowers begin to bloom.

Some flowers show off their colors early.

In spring, new plants pop out of the brown, crumbly soil and open their green leaves to the sun.

You can add texture to your drawings by using lots of tiny dots to look like soil.

The ground is covered in soft colors of purple, pink, and yellow.

What color flowers can you see where you live?

SPRING ANIMALS

Many baby animals are born in spring.

Oink! A pudgy pink pig explores the world for the first time.

Birds lay eggs in springtime.

You can create shadows with crayons.

Hold the crayon at a slant so more than the tip touches the paper. Shade from dark to light by pressing harder and softer.

Butterflies flutter from flower to flower.

This monarch has orange and black wings.

The wings on a butterfly have symmetry.

This means they look the same on each side.

Try drawing a butterfly using symmetry!

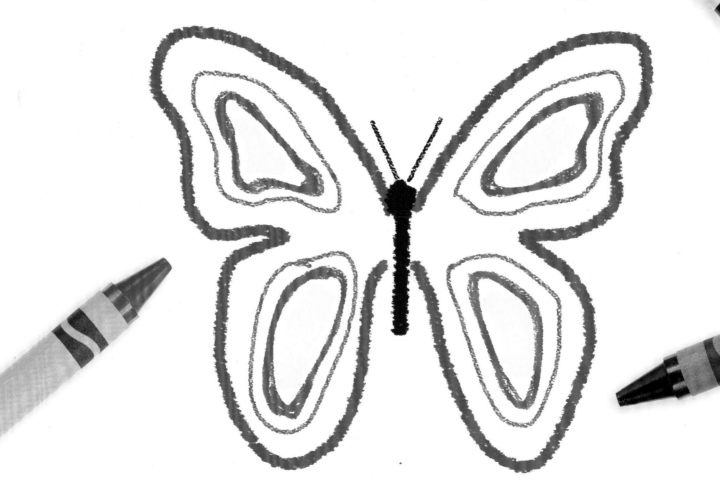

SPRING WEATHER

Splash!

Spring flowers and animals need rain. When the sun returns, a rainbow may appear!

Days grow hotter and longer.
The golden sun gets brighter.

Get ready for the colors of summer!

WORLD OF COLORS

Spring is so colorful! Here are some Crayola® crayon colors used in this book. Can you find them in the photos? What colors do you see in spring?

TICKLE ME PINK

CARNATION PINK

LAVENDER

MELON

CANARY

YELLOW

SPRING GREEN

INCHWORM

YELLOW GREEN

GRANNY SMITH APPLE

GREEN

ROBIN'S EGG BLUE

SKY BLUE

VIVID VIOLET

BEAVER

GLOSSARY

explore: to travel and look around to discover things

flutter: to move by flapping quickly, as a butterfly

pudgy: short and chubby

shade: to create a shadow

shadow: shaded area made when light is blocked

soil: the top layer of earth. Plants grow in soil.

symmetry: having two sides, or halves, that look the same

texture: the way something feels when you touch it

TO LEARN MORE

BOOKS

Brocket, Jane. *Rainy, Sunny, Blowy, Snowy: What Are Seasons?* Minneapolis: Millbrook Press, 2015. Read this colorful book to learn about all four of the seasons.

Enslow, Brian. *Spring Colors*. Berkeley Heights, NJ: Enslow, 2012. Discover more colors of spring in this fun book!

Fogliano, Julie. *When Green Becomes Tomatoes*. New York: Roaring Brook, 2016. Celebrate the seasons through the poems and illustrations of this colorful book.

WEBSITES

Butterfly Finger Puppets
http://www.crayola.com/crafts/butterfly-finger-puppets-craft/
Check out this website to design and create your own butterfly finger puppets.

Plant a Garden
http://kids.nationalgeographic.com/explore/nature/plant-a-garden
Learn how to plant a spring garden with tips from this website.

INDEX

LERNER
SOURCE™

Expand learning beyond the printed book. Download free, complementary educational resources for this book from our website, www.lerneresource.com.

PHOTO ACKNOWLEDGMENTS

The images in this book are used with the permission of: © iStockphoto.com/Moncherie, p. 1; © iStockphoto.com/stanley45, p. 2; © Smileus/Dreamstime.com, p. 5; © iStockphoto.com/Ekspansio, p. 6; © iStockphoto.com/islandgirl59, p. 7; © iStockphoto.com/bo1982, p. 8; © iStockphoto.com/zzve, p. 9 (sunflowers); © Famveldman/Dreamstime.com, pp. 10–11; © Volodymyr Burdiak/Shutterstock.com, pp. 12–13; © Lost Mountain Studio/Shutterstock.com, p. 14; © iStockphoto.com/JillLang, p. 16; © iStockphoto.com/Imgorthand, p. 19; © iStockphoto.com/Savushkin, pp. 20–21.

Cover: © iStockphoto.com/AlexRaths.